HEART'S HYDROGRAPHY

Also by Sally Ito from Turnstone Press

Alert to Glory

The Emperor's Orphans

HEART'S
HYDROGRAPHY

SALLY ITO

TURNSTONE PRESS

Heart's Hydrography
copyright © Sally Ito 2022
Turnstone Press
Artspace Building
206-100 Arthur Street
Winnipeg, MB
R3B 1H3 Canada
www.TurnstonePress.com

Turnstone Press gratefully acknowledges the assistance of the Canada Council for the Arts, the Manitoba Arts Council, the Government of Canada through the Canada Book Fund, and the Province of Manitoba through the Book Publishing Tax Credit and the Book Publisher Marketing Assistance Program.

Cover image by Gen Tsuboi.

Printed and bound in Canada.

Library and Archives Canada Cataloguing in Publication

Title: Heart's hydrography / Sally Ito.
Names: Ito, Sally, 1964- author.
Description: Poems.
Identifiers: Canadiana (print) 20220271852 | Canadiana (ebook) 20220271895 | ISBN 9780888017598 (softcover) | ISBN 9780888017604 (EPUB) | ISBN 9780888017611 (PDF)

Classification: LCC PS8567.T63 H43 2022 | DDC C811/.54—dc23

Heart's Hydrography *is a journey of a soul through the terrain of language. I dedicate this book to my children, Kenji and Seika Dyck, fellow travellers on this journey of yearning and inquiry.*

Contents

Snow Globe in the Riverbank

Creation's Crashing Wave

River in Me is Dried Up

O Anti-phons

Epilogue

HEART'S HYDROGRAPHY

Preface

For the Atheist

There will be no casting of aspersions

for the heart is a primitive organ
and it is too easy to hate.

O wicked worker of iniquity,
mine enemy, deceiver, maker of lies.

No. Instead, a marvelling at the tempered calm
of this believer in nothing

who does not fall prey to the silly, fool emotions
a god is said to inspire:

Thank you! Thank you!

Praise You!

O help! Help!

Ashamed of the dumbstruck wonder
that is my soul's need, sheepish in the tent
of faith, my glimpse of the
One who believeth not
is of admiration.

Still, this is not to denigrate
but is instead reluctant praise
from the plucked gut of a wounded animal,
of the one not yet struck,
bounding away, in leaps and strides
into the dark hills beyond the hunter's gaze;
praise for the creature, whole and without blemish,
praise for the one who needs no sacrifice.

Watery Gratitude

Holy Saturday

The sky is uncertain, clouding over one minute,
letting the sun shine the next. Its inability to choose
is a metaphor for my own lax state of belief.
Indifference is what crucified Him,
I tell my only son, while paring an apple.
What? he says. *What's indifference?*
Never mind, I reply. The light through the window
has an unsettled look, and the wind is picking up,
shaking the branches of the elm. The dog raises
its head and hears something only it can hear.
I slice the apple into quarters and give a piece to my son.
In the kitchen, a lump of dough rises
in the bread pan.

Christmas Ornament

For my daughter

I broke it, she wails, bursting into tears.

The once ancient glass orb
(the blue of Galilee)
(the silver of Judas)
is now a smattering of shards
under the tree.

This ornament came to us
secondhand, first owned by
a Catholic priest who, on retiring,
gave it to my daughter's godmother,
who then passed it on to her.

There is no point in chastening the girl.
She is already full of regret.

For she has touched the beautiful and fragile,
and been a part of its shattering.

Her cry is Mary Magdalene's; her confession
the nard of all our longing.

Motherhood

Jail sentence, a time out, spent in the corner of a life;
a squat on the stool in the boxing ring—mouth swizzled
out by water, words of exhortation from gruff-mouthed coach—
Carry on, Big Mama, ya got it in ya. You can do it, yes,
get up, push, and push back, and the light luminous that streams
through the bars in the enclosure you're in—a *life* chosen,
in fact—will fill your eyes with watery gratitude, and then when
gumption returns, you'll get up for more of the one-two fist-punch
pummel of the scrunched-up infant face wail and whine,
batter-ramming breast and bone with unformed hands while
Mommy! Mommy! Mommy! jabbing you in the ear.
None of this you will regret, you tell yourself,
the years of effort spent on this child becoming
your eventual pardon and release.

Holy Terror

Last night, I read to my daughter
the Irish legend of St. Brigid,
whose devotion to God was so utter and fearless
she plucked out her own eyeball
instead of marrying a man
whose proposal she would not, could not accept.
This was no woman of meekness, but a holy terror,
fierce and fiery in her faith. My daughter, not put off
so much by the saint's violence, is, rather,
perturbed by Brigid's annoying habit
of giving away her father's possessions
to the poor. Brigid's father is also annoyed by this habit
and complains bitterly of it to the king.
I try explaining to my daughter
that girls in medieval Ireland cannot have possessions,
and Brigid is only treating her father's things as if they were God's,
and of course, God would give away His possessions
to the poor, wouldn't He?

I want to feed my daughter stories of great saints and heroines
like St. Brigid, but frankly, such a woman terrifies me,
and sadly, I admit to myself that I do not want my daughter
to become a saint after all.

A Mother's Response

Feel free to add any additional comments on your child
on the back of this form.
                    —Church youth group registration sheet

The boy is a wonder, the apple of my eye,
a twisted ray of sunlight, ropy as a strand of silver on the tide-ebb.
He is gleam, glint, glitter—the railway on his teeth tells me so
—*I love you, Mom*—guttural in the chuff of adolescent steam
that thunders out of the teenage tank-engine heart
that is his devotion; how can I tell you more than this
in the short space of a paragraph?
The boy is my unfolding parable, paradox unowned, unexplained,
his existence slipping out of my clutches, fetters,
into some mysterious autonomy I cannot fathom.
You will shape him, I hope, God, who shaped me,
who takes the *Wassup?* hands, the *I-don't-know* shrugs,
and the *Do-You-really-exist?* questions of every generation
since Adam and holds them in Your pierced palm
the way Love does, and listens, just listens, as the heart in him
cries out for the moon, the yip yowl yearn for true light.

First Snow

On the day of first snow, a Sunday,
she lost the car keys while looking for
her daughter's winter boots, tucked in
some far corner in the basement.

Then, she remembers she threw them out
this past spring, late as it was, because
the girl had worn them out,
holes in the heels where her ankle had dug through
from the constant shoving in and out
of a growing foot in a shoulder season of snow,
sleet, and rain.

A long winter it was, and now it is here again.

With no boots for the child and missing keys,
she cannot drive to church,
nor can she walk with the daughter in the snow—
It's too late anyway, she thinks, while glancing out
the window at the bright white gathering of flakes
on that dark patch of soil that was once their garden.

Only Connect

This morning, on the windowsill,
a spider spun a silver thread
from the leaf tip of the paperwhite
all the way to the ceiling.

This morning, my cousin had a baby girl whom she named Momo.

This morning, the sermon was on the marvels of the natural world
and how we could not help but respond with awe,
with belief that behind all that design
was an intelligence, divine and sentient.

By suppertime, the silvery thread from plant
to ceiling has disappeared.
At the table, I hold the newborn Momo
while recounting the sermon to her father.

When I put my own daughter to bed that night,
I notice an old notebook
sticking out from under her toy box. In it, she has written:

Memory is when you just found out something
and you store it in your brain.

Hockey Scout

It is a dance deliberate on ice by the player
for the unknown man in the stands who is
all eye, tracking the glide and glimmer
of limb across the glassy surface.

There is an eye, too, which tracks the soul
from above, and in soul's quickened movement
finds pleasure. And while bodies lurch and dart,
such a gaze is in pursuit of glory.
For glory is this eye's realm,
in the lightning-tongue of His approval.

All parts of the living body stir under His eye,
veins of silver and gold agleam in flick and twitch,
synapse and twist of muscle and joint, waiting
to be discovered. Watched, this game
means everything, whether won or lost.

After Communion, or Giving Underage Girls Their First Drink

The wine's aftertaste is sweet, Mommy, she reports to me in the pew.
She's only eleven and she's been drinking the wine
at the rail for a year now.
Each time before that, the taste reported has been bitter.
That's why they shouldn't give kids the cup,
my ex-evangelical friend grumbles,
it's wasted on them. Nothing is wasted on children.
It is bitter, I tell her, because His death was bitter.
And she nods, understanding fully in only the way children can.
How to explain then, the sweet? His resurrection, surely?
Or our memory of loving Him,
an aftertaste of His glorious death? Whatever.

The man in the neighbouring pew tells
of his daughter's first time at the rail.
She took a sip from the cup and swooned backwards—
always the drama queen.
Forbidden for the next two Sundays and chastened,
her next approach to the rail was sober and solemn.
The father, now the chastened one,
wished he hadn't thought her drunk, or *acting* drunk,
whatever the case might have been.
For the girl had just tasted of the blood of Christ
and knew it somehow.
If she grows up to be the actress he thinks she will become,
this is the one role he will always remember her for.

Wild Plum

Her soccer practice cancelled,
we walk to the woods instead
to pick wild plums.

Leave some for the squirrels,
the daughter says absently
while minding the dog.
Each plum in the tree dangles
like a jewel from a lobe,
and like some matronly monarch
from yore, I finger them like
treasure. The treasure is time,
you see, spent with the daughter
in a careless hour of foraging
just before dusk. Soon
she will disappear like the moon
into a brooding cloud of dismay
and disappointment in me, her mother,
who shows only greediness
for these scant occasions when
the fruit is ripe and ready
for the plucking.

Ditchfuls of Wildflowers

There's nothing like ditchfuls of wildflowers
to soothe the sunset-rage of old age,
when hoar and thistle spike the gaze
with bitters, strong and bracing like regret.
Taste, that hardened witch of design,
has gone lax in her limbs, and hangs off
the broom handle, upside down like a bat
for another view of the world from where,
out of night, stars tumble into the ground
and become incarnate as blossoms in the day.
For what wildflower will you ever see again
in that same place in the ditch as the same person
you were this year? Imperfection is in the beholder
whose eyes are like mirrors, silvered with a self
that might drink with a gaze over the rim
of a goblet of the wine of all that is seen.

A Dog Poem

For Bella

That amiable darkness that is my companion,
that sits at the foot of my whirling-dervish seat
in front of the oracle screen and inter-well,
that pants, snuffles, sniffs in the just-so hours
at the leash, this god-dog muse that is, like
the writer, overweight and lonely (well and good
that she is, to bring a certain levity into the house).
What other matron might command such an audience as this?
All waggle-tail and tongue-loll, the living in her is all aquiver;
a shelter dog, she has a past but does not dwell in it;
her joy and happiness is wordless; one can read all the poetry
of the world to her and she will not know its pleasure,
but her love is certain—this is what her kind
has been bred for, and we, too, if only we knew it.

49th Year

This year has been a battleground—husband lost to cancer,
father to a hematoma due to a fall, neighbour to stroke. Alone,
in your half-renovated house (for he died too soon to complete it),
you grieve. Death, suffering. This is the stuff of 49.
A bad luck year, say the Japanese. Four is *shi*—death.
And nine is *ku* for *kurushimu*—suffering.
Death comes in threes, it's true. And in one year, you are
widowed, orphaned, and unfriended. But wait. Turn around.
There is light in the window, in the studio he built for you.
Love in the meals he once made of your still favourite foods,
and then photos of the things you did together—
the travelling, the hiking and biking. The wooden bowl
he made for you fills with tears of remembrance
which is all we have, alas, to stem the tide of time
that will sluice clean the bowl, make it empty once again.

Dervish

Grumble-puss and consternation, maudlin matron is at the helm,
tears like crumbs at the plate's edge, running down
the dry cheeks' plain of daily existence—
that pored, age-spotted prairie—skin's chagrin at getting old.
Something and everything frustrates—lost mittens by kittens,
the *What's-for-supper?* madness of a ravenous, crow-haired teen,
the *I-can't-find-it* look of the husband
who probably wants something younger, more tender, more juicy
than the hunk of flesh you slap on the plate for him.

Servitude no longer suits.
Submission is the will you have no stomach for.
You enter the Pause like a dervish
about to set fire to the wick of longing,
the hunger that has not been met
by your burrowing away of idylls and reveries you call poetry,
when all the words do is gasp and start
like a choked engine, sputterings out of the throat.

Bleeding Woman

Take heart, your faith has made you well.
—Matthew 9:22

Blanched, the womb. For years, shedding the ruby lining,
the clots and lumps of blood; the reddish clay of her crumbling
a curse far worse than death. She is desperate.
Clinging, cloying to the cloth, anyone that might
sop up the spillage, she reaches out one last time,
determined. It is for this reaching that He lives,
turns, and gives the word. It is for this reaching,
yes, for all.

The County Fair

is the confluence of all human appetite
for the bounty of the harvest, the thrill of a
carnival ride, the sugar-sweet of confection.
In the maw of a dragon, behind the curve
of its teeth, is the fairground stage, the spokes of
the Ferris wheel, with its cogitating concentricity,
the up-and-down roller coaster,
the tawdry lights of the midway,
its multitude of amusements. Soon, its
temporary abode on the monster's tongue
will be finished, and it will disappear
into the dark throat of autumn, whose rising moon,
like the eye of the dragon, glows
with satisfaction at a meal well consumed
as it wings its serpentine body in search of heaven.

Midwaist in the Shallows

Prow

When it smoothly pressed its way
through green and yellow lily pads,
the canoe felt to me like church—
its upside-down roof of a boat's bottom
sailing me to heaven while I sang
hymns under its rafters.

Drifting into the calm of unknown waters,
I wonder, do I know this place?

Deer and I

Once a year, Deer and I meet—
usually on the side of the road—
and we have our ritual exchange
of fear and wonderment
before parting.

Startled by each other's presence,
we become unintended deities
to one another, as if sent.

The rest of the year is spent forgetting,
sentience slipping into the sleep
of self-absorption

only to be awakened again
suddenly

by this encounter, brief
as the moon's face in a dreamer's pond.

Vesper Sparrow

Grey and brown, streaked with black
like the dusk before the bars of night
settle into the score, it is named for
singing more melodiously at night,
though who knows if it was ever really heard
singing in the morning's racket.

Voice text:

Here, here, where, where. Hisp.

Quick to inhabit abandoned sites
of human activity—old mines, forgotten farms—
it sings in groups known as
'congregations' or 'liturgies' of its kind.

Attracted to its name, I, too, call out for it
as I do, a lover
in the language of a bard of my kind.

Where, wherefore art thou?

Nation of Birds

What if our only home were the air
and our wings flapping through it?
And time the space we lived in,
and the nest, a current for our eggs?

What if there were no abode but
shore or field, one day to the next—
the wide sky, the only true resting place
made of movement and yearning
for a never arriving home?

Husk

The milkweed on its stalk in autumn opens;
the brown-seeded eyes gaze outward to the sky.
Soon the wind will scoop out the feathery gossamer,
setting the seeds aloft, afloat into the world.

And what of the empty husk now?

It becomes grotto, cradle, or bark, some
vessel of imagining—a shelter for the Virgin,
a bed for the Christ Child, a boat for
the fleeing Holy Family.

How the busy mind aches
to fill the emptiness
with story, that rattling abode of air
in which seeds once dwelled.

Forge

For death is no more than a turning of us over from time to eternity.

—William Penn

The autumn tree is a forge, the fire-flicker flames
licking at the long-limbed branches, making them
red-hot in the waning days of this season's light.
Eventually, the branch cools, hardens, becomes black.
And then, when frost arrives, its silver coats and plates
the bony, pointing arms with their sword-tip barbs,
to make them javelins to pierce the darkness of the heavens—
that carcass from which the spirit of the sun has already fled.
But I am still here, caught in the web and stickiness of Time.
I have not entered that fire yet. The fog from my lungs
is a mist I breathe out, and like steam off the freshly
defecated, a sign of the stench of me, that consumer of the
world's wonders in the shutter-ball that is the eye, in the print-press
of the brain, the forge that fires the type and gives name and word
to stuff that might eternal be,
if only for the one who reads and remembers.

Confused Willow

A warm spell in February, and the confused willow,
thinking spring might be here, opens its spear bud,
pokes out grey fur—a rabbit's foot, thrust out for luck.
And now that it's out, it cannot go back in, the joey's head too big
for the sheath, the pouch, that once held it.
Will it die, you think, for being too bold, rash, and unwary?
It has only temperature and light with which to gauge itself.
And now comes regret, the sting of shame,
for having hoped too much.
A silly optimist, this willow bud.
But someone has noticed this tip of grey, blessed it with her gaze
as she might an old woman's head, at the desperate edge of a pew,
kneeling with her to give a tender word. Poet or priest, she is called.

Winter Haiku

January

Resolute

Winter joggers and bikers
make progress
on snowy roads

*

Sundogs circling the sun
Fingertips around a whitehead

*

Looking for the moon
in the pale morning sky
like I would in my fingernail

*

Lake Ice

What mirror of words
might reflect this art?

February

DANGER: THIN ICE sign
in the middle of the river—
who put you there?

*

The amaryllis is
giving the finger
to winter

*

Warm Spell

Creek a muddled yellow
unable to decide whether
to freeze or melt

*

Mindfulness

How to walk the path
without slipping on ice

*

Last day of February
Shrove Tuesday
Geese on river ice

March

Blizzard Rumours

Glittering snowflakes
swarm like white gnats
on the back deck

*

Howling wind outside
I hear you
What do you want?

Ice Formations on Winnipeg Beach, January 2017

*Conditions never seen before on this stretch of lakeshore have made for
eerie formations of ice and snow.*

—Newspaper Report

Teats and testicles, stalactites and stalagmites
pucker and purse, pustule and pimple,
dreadlocks and dynamite sticks,
a waterspout or tornado, all frozen, of course
—the eye mouthing meaning
into each unnamed, icy protuberance
as if you are running a finger over
a dill pickle, or humming a tune,
rubbing the udder before milking.

And what of the holes in the ice,
big enough to shelter in?
Grotto, cave, cell—
the words ring religious,
as if your presence in them is a bell clapper,
a stone in the well, plopping in the pond
of a frozen mind.

Who in this place has sought refuge or mercy,
you wonder, been blessed by the wan light above
leaking through the hole in the ice where framed
are flights of birds, silhouettes of trees,
the stars, and the moon?

Is this God's embrace, the ascetic's ecstasy?

I do not know. But to get in
you must stoop and kneel,
creep and crawl creaturely
into the shiny, studded maw of ice
and dwell for a moment as if wholly consumed
by cupped waters that will soon melt
back into an inchoate sea.

Walking on Water

What winter makes possible—
walking on water, springtime's gush quelled
into sheets of ice; in Death's season, such are the miracles.
No one believes this miraculousness, so ordinary it is—
the foot crunch of the pathfinder made steady
by a vein of liquid now hardened into
rigid roadway. Walking every day in winter is a resolution
and calls for determination. *Overcoming* is a word
best suited to those who braved the icy land bridge in its
coldest hour to set foot on a continent hitherto unknown.
Those who seek will find, was it not promised?
And everyday miracles will be part of the discovery
of the soul's newest terrain.

In Spring, Winter Believes

In spring, winter believes.
It's a faith hard-won in the cold, frozen
Ground-of-Being; there's certainty, nonetheless,
of a thawing, a breaking, a fracture
in the ice. For always embedded in this ground
are seeds. Therein lies the mystery. For who
planted the seed but God the Human, sowing
among the furrows the kernel of today's longing
for the certainty of tomorrow?

Bathymetrics

A term for sounding the depths of waterways,
measured by a person with a stick wading incrementally
into waters, like a man or woman rationally testing the faith
before full-immersion baptism.

Bathymetrics becomes metaphor for unlike things—
one's soul the river, the measuring stick, a personal accounting
of the water's level, its edge when shallow climbing up the body
until the body disappears, consumed by the riverine soul-waters,
who can't stop measuring even when submerged.
Isn't the stiff wooden pole, the cross that is both staff and spear,
a better instrument? my friend the preacher says,
Bible in hand, midwaist in the shallows
on the other side, awaiting your arrival.

God of the Sparrows

Today, God is in the flesh of sparrows,
      in the marrow of their song.

I catch His presence in a fleeting glance,
      even among other competing tendrils
of spring—tulip pikes and tipped branch spears—
      weaponry amassed for
the sun's shock-and-awe blast of spring
      that is His greater show.

      But the birds have lasted all winter,
endured the cold with nothing but feathers
      and hollow bones.

Their chatter in the dead season
      has sustained much
when all else had fled or perished.

This God I can worship, I think,
      this God of the sparrows.

Albino Hummingbird

Blessed are those who have not seen and have believed.

—John 20:29

Do you believe in God? she asked,
hovering over the morning glory
and the scarlet runner bean.

I do.

Believe, then, in me, she said, and flew away.

Wildflower

Nameless thing,
small and red,
dangling from a stem.

What are you?

Nameless one,
with whom I have slept
and wed.

Who are you?

An Invasive Species of Doubt

On Easter Sunday, on the back table at the church,
a stack of full-colour pictorial calendars issued by the government:
Prairie Invasive Species: Combining Forces on Unwanted Invaders.

In the calendar are photographs of everything
from beetles to fish, grasses and flowers—
some so spectacularly beautiful as to be breathtaking
(they have already seduced the photographer).
Yet, the text spells it out clearly: *these are DEADLY*
to the natives and will CHOKE them out,
KILL them all, if given half the chance.

The Church and the Government
are the combined forces this day to combat
unwanted invaders of nature on our prairie souls.

That night, in a dream, words creep out of the brain—
Irrepressible Nihilism and Joyous
walk hand in hand in the fields—
and I am startled awake at the thought,
the words so clever, so given, so memorable
that even if I do not write them down right away,
they have already reproduced themselves in a poem by morning.

Overnight, the thistly flower has taken over the meadow,
the strange guppy-eyed fish proliferated in the lake,
the beetle bored through a bark unprepared for its kind.

And so I live with these invasions of the soul daily,
my shutter-eye glad of their insouciant, aggressive beauty.
For they live to make me die, die, and one day, rise again.

The Jesus Bug

walks on water—pond skater, water strider—
and preys on the just-fallen-in,
the desperate insects out of their most rational element
—the air or web of their smug comfort—
into unfamiliar and uncommon terrain
like fear or wonder whose name is *aqua*—
a surface under which lie great depths;
the face of faith exhibits this demeanour, for example,
in the way our tears and smiles can be skated on
in an easy religious interpretation of events
when something far more complex is going on.

Gerridae is a family of true bugs in the order Hemiptera, commonly known as water striders, water bugs, magic bugs, pond skaters, water scooters, water skaters, water skeeters, water skimmers, water skippers, water spiders, or Jesus bugs.

Contemplating the Raspberry
in the Convent Garden

The mortal clots in the jam-jar heart are berry-red
and every pustule of blood sings sweet its squinch,
cries brokenness. This many-chambered crimson hive
is Your dwelling place, and the seed encumbered within,
engorged in its casing of gel, will one day ensure
another brambled stalk of its kind in this garden of devotion,
tended for the fruits of its vines, Your words dangling
from this measured line.

Tomatoes

Brandywine (Sudduth's Strain)

This year's misshapen varieties remind one of a drunkard's nose,
Venus of Willendorf, sex and genitals. The fruit, cracked
and bulbous, are the sweetest ever—salted and sucked
until nothing is left but wet skin. But the seeds have been saved,
so there'll be more next year, planted in anticipation—a lover
strewing the bed with devotion and longing. This carnal
grotesque in the basket is more alluring than any of the other
pincushion-perfect orbs, for it has drunk of the wine of sunlight
and fattened itself on midsummer rains. It begs to be held, cradled,
and fondled from out of the summer kiln of its baking—
and the master will marvel at what the fire has wrought
on the ware, the fruit of creation.

Marsupial Vision

That line of sight from out of the hearth-pocket of Mother
tells of a world out there.
Inside the fur walls is Mother's heartbeat,
like the drum-throb, pulse-ache of the pausarius
urging the oar-arm thrust into the waters,
to push ahead to the finish line, that *ta-da* to end the *te-dums*.
Now with head and forepaws out, the drawstring pouch
will keep safe its soul-currency, blinking and juddering,
up and down, the flash and flutter of its gaze
against the haze and dust of moving Mother—
great globe she is—carrying *us* on her suspension-built legs
meant to bounce, bounce, the heart ball up, up
into skies of praise
and down, down to earth again.

Rooster Song

Resurrection is a rooster song, pulling dawn
out of the ground like the early bird it is,
and all that is earth in you will feel daylight
on droop-darkened hill, on withered-as-grass burdened shoulders.
Only the winged and raucous can arouse the living
from death-sleep, awaken the Peter-person
who has thrice denied and, in repentance
for wilful ignorance, marks the fiery hackles
of the cock's crowing body like a noose
that tightens with conviction your throat 'til you, too, must cry out,
He lives, He lives, Christ Jesus lives today.

Organ

The bowels of the church. Its guts and bellows.
Mass pipeline. Pump and squeeze,
praise throttled out into cavern of grandeur, the hallow house.
Hoary, frost-haired *organiste* in soft soles
peddling, paddling the bowed-roof ark to the shores
of glory and back. The praise plumber forcing air
and pulling knobs, rendering the fat of church coffers
to oil the lamps of hearts' devotion.

Sometimes there is no music in the house; deep down
in the ground, the pipes are frozen with regret or layered with
the sediment of unholy, listless days. The pipes are jail bars.
Imprisonment. But then,
The wind bloweth where it listeth and thou hearest
the sound thereof.
And a groaning begins, the flesh muttering itself alive.
What spark is to flame, what spittle is to sight,
pitch, tone, and key reunite, reignite, channelling the blast
of fiery air through pipes once more. This is the mystery
of our melting, this season into heartspring,
the organ song, a reawakening.

The Moon to the Mountain

I love you, said the moon to the mountain
I love you, said the mountain to the lake
I love you, said the lake to the wind
I love you, said the wind to the tree
I love you, said the tree to the bird
I love you, said the bird to its young
I love you, said the young to the mother

I love You, said the poet to the Word
Word sighed, and said, *It is finished.*

Snow Globe in the Riverbank

Snow Globe

I dreamt I found a snow globe
in the riverbank, and inside its glassy orb,
another globe. In that one, I was digging through another bank—
this time of snow—as if that other I
would never find myself in time.

I awoke before I could pick up the globe,
and that was when I wrote this down. Strangely,
I remember not the image, for there was none—
just the word *snow globe* pressed upon
the mind like a heavy paperweight,
insisting I write it down and make of it
a poem.

Verse Hung Up

Verse hung up, you are, lilac-snatcher of the alleys,
out in the wee hours of bird wake and whistle,
prowling for beauty. Sprig, twig, and spray
alert you to the line, where end-stop buds the blossom.

This valiant searching, this wonder-predation
on the trees' transitory, the season's sporadic
is as cat to bird—your poet hand the paw that might descend
on flight, squash its fleetingness
to make out of it word-pies and poesy-tarts
et posterum, for God's sake, make art.

Pessimilitude

Don't write. Don't ever write. No one
will ever read your stuff. Be prepared
for rejection. One in ten acceptances for publication
is the norm. No one cares. Least of all your children.
They are in the next room watching television
or playing video games on the computer.
Bake a cake. The satisfactions for excellent baking
are more easily digested. Forget poetry.
If literature is strong medicine, no one really
takes it unless they are dying, and even then
some will reject its balm and die anyway.

Fatalist

Journalists beheaded, children enslaved,
a country overrun by tanks.

And if my poetry purports to care, it doesn't really.

Every day, I beat my head on a gong of meaninglessness
to drown out the sound of the world's despair.

I *wish* I could care.

O Lord, help thou my unbelief!

Distractions

Lord, free me from my imagination,
from the seethe and coil, hiss and snap
of words, their entanglement a nest
of the infinitely possible.
Stay my hand from the chocolate box
of words that for only seconds
feeds the heart with sweetness and despair.
Not even for myself, but for others
to whom I thrust the box, the bouquet,
saying, *Love me for my words, for I have loved you.*
A carnal harlot, a pin-up poster gal
compels desire, carmine to the eye,
caramel to the lip, everything gazed on—
a feast of words to be consumed utterly,
then regretted.

Evergreens, or
The Lordship of the Language

In spaces and hollows, on ledges and lumps,
the evergreens hold the snow, their barbed
and pointed branches arrowing down the cold air,
shoulders mantled with the mottled and matted
ermine-skin of kingship. A circle of them, upright
from the ground, form the spikes of a foreign crown
that in my night's dream sits uneasy on the brow,
and tells me how I might rule over winter with my words.
I don't know how, I cry out, and awaken to see
a tree's slim silhouette under the lamplight,
as someone awaiting a crown, full-skirted
in a gown's array of tumbling silks, and I fear I cannot see her,
nor any of her kind, except as monarchs,
whirling in the mind's accursed mythologies
where trees are not trees, but rulers instead of me,
shackled by this language's clanking armoury
into an obeisance, unbecoming, and not truly free.

Haiku on the same trees:

Snow on evergreens
curved like an eyelash,
fringed with white seeing.

Autumn's Canopy

Autumn's canopy is a constellation of star-leafed decay,
each a comet ablaze in its own dying, soon to fall from the
dark-treed universe of its unfurling; this must be the way
we enter the world and leave it, too. This fiery array is a diadem
on the wrinkled brow of matron Earth, and you, beneath it,
middle-aged and with the frost already in your hair,
look up and perceive in the stars some portent of your future—
some distant glory in this un-veining of the sun-catcher,
whose shrivelling and withering art is not unlike your own
burning of life's coal into the pencil-lead ash of poetry.

Unnavigable

Into this unnavigable floats a babe in a basket.
A tributary begins where muck meets water, enough
to succeed in drowning anything weighted or heavy.
The babe in the basket is the Moses-soul, the one who
will be delivered, and deliver also. The basket is a vessel
and the vessel is language. It is the woven intention of words
meant for holding, carrying, cradling. It is conveyance.

Am I the babe, or the basket? Is the marsh the beginning
of Time's river, or its end? Who has set whom on the waters
of what place, what moment? Into the paradox of being,
I walk this poem as if it were a dog to the water's edge
where it loses the scent and paces the bank in confusion.

Eyehole

Through the eyehole of the word, *me* is gazed.
Through fired glass, a glimpse of clay,
slowed time and I together
rocking in the sound-sense waves of day.
Ship and sea in the porthole
are also, me.

Life Beyond Word

How to glimpse it without burnishing it into *be-ing*.
How to grasp it incarnationally.
How to recognize without knowing.

Nameless it might start, but even then,
once spoken, has passed through the air,
an object thrown by a subject.

Convince—The Evangelist's Task

Convince and possess them, that is the evangelist's task—
to take the living as convicts, cuff and shackle them,
make them do the Lord's bidding. For after all, at his
Repent has he not had at them? Were they not redeemed
at his reaping of them, their sickled souls in hand? He is
their Bethlehem-boder, star-fetcher
to their blank, meaningless lives;
he brings news of a saviour for those who want saving
from their comfortable doubt: *Is that all there is?*

But strangely, I stand with him.
I, too, want this poem to mean
like a drill in the heart,
mosquito boring through the iron bowl
called soul, your mystic consciousness, O Reader.
I want the words to drive the satori-bound train
to the Christ-Child destination through that vast desert
of your secret longing, your wanting and fearful loneliness.

Sermonica

To play the pipe of words and be not in
dull obedience to them, make poetry your art
of exhale, exhort, extol, exalt.

Rally the words, corral them into courts of praise;
make gallant your attempts to woo
—with wonder and consternation—
your abstruse confusions, your startled
revelations, your mulling meditations.

Affix the Collar, and like God's dog,
bark, yap, and yowl (but unlike a cur,
neither snap nor snarl), and raise your head
to hear heaven's Invisible, lower snout to ground
to snuffle-nuzzle the earth.

Oh, but then doubt strikes its gong
and the head swirls and swivels in confusion.
Why instruct at all? Why make them listen?
Of mortal misgiving I am mostly made,
and thus play words to proclaim:
language is a creature you cannot tame.

Love Consists of Sentence Translations

Love consists of sentence translations,
as if one by one, each word, like a bird, flies into
the hand of the other. Fragrance knows no
other self but the word that describes it
when it wafts through the air, signalling the presence
of the beloved. This body is a letter—
it opens, and like a sonnet with wings,
declarative, announces with a voice
the unseen particles of affection in a vibrating hum
of matter that is the realm of the psychic and invisible.

Before Pentecost is Ordinary Time

Between the blooming of the lily of the valley
that grows in the shadows of trees,
and the bright burst of the peony's orb
into an open palm in sunlight, is Ordinary Time.

This is the hour before the vow is made,
the hour before a decision to end a life or make a new one,
the hour with or without a book, the hour of idle waiting.
In this hour, nothing occurs, and everything.

Imagine a room with everyone in it. Waiting and praying.
Imagine you in it. *But,* you protest,
this is the world we live in every day.
No. Not yet.

Houndstooth

Houndstooth. Its jagged pattern in suit jackets
and trousers and skirts. The word hounds me
and will not let go of imagination's leg. It has dug
in deep and affects my walking, my journeying
day to day in this soul-park of being. I wonder why
I've been made captive by this heaven hound, this dog
of the Goya painting, parked in the middle of a vast, formless
sand of yellow, its ears perked up, eyes alert.
It has heard the call of mystical nonsense and then bitten
my leg to tell me of it. Now I limp and stagger, trying to find
a name for it—not the dog, but its wounding—
and it is *houndstooth*. Houndstooth is all I have in my
coin purse/arsenal/letterbag of words for things
seen and yet also unseen.

Creation's Crashing Wave

Comfort Words

In homage to Catharina Regina von Greiffenberg

How her comfort words, they attack me. Scatter
the doubt like hard pellets of shot in the thickening air
of dusk. I am like that wounded thing, fearful and almost defeated,
panting in the bush. Someone staunch the blood.
It trickles and oozes.

Her faith, worthy-earned by her zealous words, overwhelms
and I, wanting to flee, clamp down on the bit—
glory, power, might, strength—the words of her arsenal,
a heraldic chorus, a festooning of the bridle-metal
of this woman's utterings. Its silver will rein me in,
its conviction jail me behind piety's gleaming bars.

*Catharina Regina von Greiffenberg was a seventeenth-century Austrian devotional poet.

Winter's Eden

Inspired by Catharina Regina von Greiffenberg

In this winter's Eden, when the eyes are lined with
the salt rime of tears, lo, a flower blooms in
all that blasts and blinds. Unfolding its petals, hour by hour
in this world-womb of woe, it stops time and with its fruit
ushers in the old garden made new.

As with a plain of newly fallen snow after a storm,
Heaven's ice will gleam and glitter there.
And our footfalls will go backwards from
their stray blue wanderings to the cross-piece,
that flower-fingered, piercèd hand that has lit
this wick of longing and brought light into darkness,
like Him who into the sky brings in the orb that makes
day out of night.

Word Sculptor

Inspired by Catharina Regina von Greiffenberg

In the material of Your language do I carve out praise
with the hammer of my right to the chisel of my left.
What woman could hold such tools without Your strength in her?
Your Word is the marble's soul which my sculptor's hand must
reveal. I must paint the ceiling of my gaze
with Your earthly presence. For this cathedral of word-wonder,
this sonnet of praise is the house of all my longing.

Take root in the stone as a vein of gold, quicken it
with Your Holy Spirit so that it flickers and flames,
turning the unliving into the living.
And when all arm strength is spent
and scant are the words, line-lift the wings to guide-glide
my hands into their destined harbour, that place of arrival,
not of my will but of Yours, come in O Lord.

Wonder-Praise

Inspired by Catharina Regina von Greiffenberg

What is this wonder-praise that comes out of me?
How dare the mouth and pen attempt the unattemptable?
Yet I cannot help it, cannot stay the hand, nor clamp shut
the valve of singing that is my heart's desire.

You cannot help then but wonder-bless me!
Me, the deceiving Jacob, the undeserving
who puts out my arms, cloaked in the sheepskin
of Your son's redeeming.

Bless me, I say, reward me for my audacity;
even if I must vie with the angels for eternity,
nothing is worth living for but to praise You endlessly.

Spring is Earth's Language for Praise

Inspired by Catharina Regina von Greiffenberg

Spring is Earth's language of praise to God—
resurrection green from out of the old, exposed brown
of a wound once scabbed over, now bleeding with life
in cornets and trefoils, petalled and bejewelled.
Who needs our miserable words when His own chorus
sings with the winds and waters of the world?
He will praise Himself. But for us, niggling in our need,
He concedes the language of the stars, stuffs the cosmos
down our throats until we gag on its immensity,
spit out our insignificance. *Lo, You are the Almighty,*
we sputter to say, even if He doesn't have to hear it.
And if the daffodils sway away from us to Him, so be it,
the bright ones know truly whom they worship.

Nephesh/Throat

Ah-dam, mud guy, is it true your *being* in Hebrew
means *living throat*—one who suckles for eternity
at God's breast? Whose thirst and hunger is this tunnel
out of which desire, craving, want, and need are constant?
Ah-dam, out of which awe, ah, oh, are uttered
with gape, gulp, swallow to follow—and then from within,
cry-fly, moan-groan, yip-yap spirit-song out of the
praise-grate of the heart? Clay vessel with a hole,
pipe-tube built for yearn and yodel, you are essentially
passage to and fro, through dirt-darkness—train chuffing steam,
progress of the will in and out to stations
of glory and back.

Of the Pure and Primitive Devotion
of Bishop Lancelot Andrewes

Had you seen the Original Manuscript, happy in the glorious
deformity thereof, being slubbered [stained] *with His Pious hands,*
and watered with His penitential tears, you would have been forced
to confess That Book *belonged to no other than pure and Primitive*
Devotion.
                    —Richard Drake, in the first printed edition (1684)

Let us commit pen to the page's white brightness,
and then let the page be sodden, besotted with heart's
grudge-gratitude to that which has broken through, the leak
in the damming, discerning vision that seeks always truth,
pure and simple, simple and pure. Truth, not anti-truth.

The good Bishop cried when he wrote his words on prayer.
And Creation's crashing waves limned the lower lid,
and broke over the stone wall of his reticence, of his
encumbrance, and the words moved out of him, through
that tunnel, the echo chamber of desire, sluicing into the
Garden, watering the plants of all reading peoples.

Cinquains for Love

In homage to George Herbert

Submit
to the Form, I
will to You whom Love is
and all encompass, eternal
manna

*

O Spring,
in whom Love lives,
a blossom unfolding,
temporal bliss this petall'd kiss
of life

*

Summer,
when Love's leaf'd hand
reveals the sacraments
of light, water, to give, receive
blessing

*

Autumn,
when Love's piercèd
side bleeds in chalices
brimming red with the harvest wine
of grief

*

Winter
is Love longing
for the Beloved, buried
under snow's cold indifference,
waiting

Breath-Skill

That man, he has breath-skill, born a word-worship he was;
rides the bard barge boldly, rhyme shoots the rapids
with his tongue-tack, held 'twixt teeth like sail
through song-stress sibilance, wonder in its wake;
earth crack and sea swell, throat thunder threshing
honey harvest halcyon, all hours 'til gloaming, his
pulse-praise penetrates, bangs the ear-hear drum,
sprouts out from sound-drought, shill song sheaves
glory grains gained and ghosted, kings feted and bested
in voice-vain veritas, told in Time's tell-tempoed grip
until death's dark dagger, night's knight slays him.

The Sister

Fair fresh this face, filing faithfully through
the hallowèd hall all hidden.
And though this maid be mirror-mistress
of gaze-blessing gentleness and quiet countenance,
vision vanity is not hers, nor blinded by her beauty-burden
is she, who shine-shapes inwardly the inner sinner of Christ's
dinner guest, begrimed and guilty, unable to take her hosting hand
but for her welcome-words. For with her walks Love and Light,
and tender-telling is her speech, soft with praise-purpose poise
as she glides graceful across the floor, fluid and faithful
to the melt-moult music of her woo-wealth words,
plentiful in prayerful practice, to friend the friendless,
fledge them into flowering, grow them into goodness.

River in Me is Dried Up

Heart's Hydrography

Those meanderings of the soul, how they
spout or sputter, bubble and froth.
There is deluge and flood, and then the Sea,
that undulating womb of water
in which infant me is wafting. The poet Catharina
channels, restrains, controls the flow of
churlish water winding its way through
the heart's time-terrain to saturate devotion's soil
with prayer-present wave after wave of words.

The river in me is dried up. No longer capable of melt or sorrow.
What happened to Gethsemane's tears—
its salt water turned to blood?
Why are they not in me? To bring me back to that Sea
which we *in spiritus sanctus* once were and still wish to be?

Pantry

In front of the pantry cupboard of moments, you pause to decide
which memory is worth retrieving for the day's writing.
There are those things you used to crave: the languorous kiss
like a tin of oysters nestled in oil,
or something sugary and whimsical
as newly blown snow on the snuffle-jowls of the dog,
or maybe a stack of crackers—some interminable tower of time
during which ideas appeared layered as sustenance, but later
prove unsatisfactory. The older you get, the more the mind fills,
and the salt and sugar you used to desire so much out of life
crumble, seep, trickle into a muddle of uncertainty until
you are left scratching your head, wondering more about that
dark hole in the back where rodents dart in and out,
stealing time and energy in their mere scurry to survive.
Soon the mysterious entryway to that hole will be yours
and you will disappear into its darkness
with nary a morsel of memory.

Sabotage

Sabotage with Saviour Fuel, this trunk-thick torpor
of mine; pump it in sideways in the gash below the rib,
just under the heart, where it all began, this energy-for-living
become energy-for-sinning. Circulate the new blood
into the old bag-skin 'til body bursts, and flesh-freed is
the soul as if spit out, the wide arc of its trajectory
like a shooting star in the darkness of being
—visible and radiant—this brief eternity that spins
the cosmos with its otherworldly hope of arrival.

Monocrat

Deceived by reason, you are unable to submit to wonder.
The foolish deserve forgiveness, but you don't,
and are proud. Everything aches with meaning and longs
for your embrace, but you are cold and indifferent.
Prayer might chisel a chink in the armour, but likely not,
for who will pray for you but someone perverse and persistent
—a love martyr—who knows no reward except your bewildered
presence in Heaven? And then you will think, bitterly,
that God has won, and sink like a stone into Hell, victorious.

Idle

in the pew as in life, awaiting deliverance from this dullness
that is all exhort and exhaust; where, O Salvation, art thou?
Sometimes it comes in the fist-cherub face of the bawling infant's
cacophonous interruption, crow squawk to the sermon song,
insisting on milk and crumbs in the ever present *Now*
that is your idle alertness. Waiting, it seems, is a ponderous affair
and you have no time for it, this idleness that is the only state
that permits of dream, scheme, and imagine. And yet,
you are nonetheless here in the pew, attending the urge to
connect with world's soul-weathers, its weal and woe
sometimes your own, you must admit. You are that car in park,
idling, engine humming, nowhere to go and that is as it should be,
you chastise yourself, squirming and ungrateful in your praise.

Sacrament

Babe in a manger, in the creature trough,
meant to be consumed and chewed on,
your swaddled seed-pod body will
soon be grain-ground into powder
by the millstones of rolling time.
On my rough tongue, you, too, will rest
and be consumed, over and over again.
Dumb beast that I am, lowing,
to feed myself on the mystery.

Salvator Mundi—The Christ Child and I

I

Curly-headed Christ Child, already sitting upright,
hand firmly on the globe, or resting his elbow on it;
smug, you think. Predestined to die, the boy
already looks heroic, the chubs of fat around his
arms and thighs rippling like premature muscles.
He who holds the globe in his lap like a ball
will save us all with his dying. Of this, the artist
is convinced. (Me, I'm not so sure.)

II

Curly-headed Christ Child, why is the road to adore you
so narrow? *Reason, distaste, posterity* grow like weeds
around a stagnant pond, threatening to choke the channel
of praise that once flowed freely, calmly, and without obstacle
from once *Jesus-loves-me-this-I-know* lips.
Curse the self that has grown tumorous and charged, a ball
meant to acquiesce and absorb, not react and repel.
You are a miracle, why not concede it? So it is,
I see now why the artist has made you heroic. Your
muscled arms must take up the ball, *mundi*, and hurl
it hard and fast, pitcher on the mound, to break me.

Sanctification

Some burning, some sloughing off, some scraping is required,
bowing, kneeling, praying
some cleansing, bleaching, scrubbing
repent, confess, resolve
before the wax, polish, and shine.

This dull metal heart-slug, soul-stained and sin-tarnished,
can be blood-redeemed if penitent—*Let's hope!* we say
before the dunk, dip, plunge-dive into
acid baths and soapy waters, tubs and basins
of Galilee seas and river Jordans.

Something arises—silvery ash flakes
to reveal, at the bottom,
the purified and holy, at last.

Bless

Blessed be the broken, blighted, and plain old rotten;
blessed be the light that shines on the blemish,
the light that burnishes and tarnishes. Blessed be
the time in which these imperfections dwell and then perish.
Blessed be those who are cursed, and blessed be
those who will not abandon them, nay, who will
not turn away, nor flinch, nor wince. Bruised and
blighted, they are this earth's pounded clay. Pinched,
made sore, and wanting, they are not just them. But us.

Water Sermon

If out of water, I might boil into steam, longing
—pressurized breath that whistles while it works—
I might be pastor-peddling too much hot air to bear witness—
where you, most adverse, might feel only the burn of it.

Who, anyway, wants to swallow clouds? Those trace vapours
that fill up the sky with the meaningless fluff of praise?
Someone out there might yet convince you there is a god.
But not me. For this heart-heated water turns only into steam
and never into wine. My voice is not pulpit-pith but vain-vessel
for the weak and dilute; what fiery conviction ignites in others,
I but dampen with a hiss, coals of darkness and dissolution.

But if from outside this glass chamber of myself,
you might witness some alchemy—
some sublimation of word
from out of the weakness that I am—it is enough.

A Brighter Strange

The brighter strange lurks beneath sunset's rim,
its glow diffuse as arrows in a cauldron of molten iron,
its green embers the flecked ash of fallen sunlight
through a canopy of trees. This brighter strange
that seeps and scampers, no partner to shadow or shame,
exists somewhere in that flat terrain of someone else's belief
and is all they live for, you think.
Uncertain of your own state of broken light,
splintered and in shards,
emitting its own fractured reflection,
it summons the brighter strange of others.

Listen Hotel

At the Listen Hotel, the pillows are ears,
downy and tufted—holes of the wise—
in which your pebbled tears of grief and woe
might nestle for a moment, or two.

At the Listen Hotel, the view is placid,
that dark chamber beneath the lid, where
the eye lies, for once, recumbent as it does
only in death and sleep.

At the Listen Hotel, you think it is you who
needs to be listened to, but rather, it is you
who must learn to listen—listen as an
animal does—alert and aware of its existence
for the first time. Sentient, at last.

Van Gogh's Ear

What does it hear now of its own loss
in a painting meant to be seen,
not heard?

It is a shell off in the distance
from which the waves of the sea
might be heard.

In the moist, severed folds of skin
is the story of an angry disciple, a sword,
and the healing touch of a messiah.

Through its waxy cartilage, pink light
of a setting sun, or the opaque red of a burn
from being out too long on a hot summer day
painting furiously.

And in it, too, the faint, invisible praise of stars
in the night, glowing radiantly in that
vast, indifferent harmony of the cosmos.

Paintings are seen, not heard. True.
But there is still music
in broken instruments. And the ear, cut off,
still hears it.

Thrum

The begetting of sound.
The whirr of wings.
The certainty of words.

Hummingbird, thrumming.

Being stoked in the furnace of the eye,
flint spark-start of fire, descending,
then hovering, then away.

A visitation, so perfect
no one sees, only hears of
afterwards.

Pentecost.

Longing

For when the hour was baroque and there was
a fearful studied symmetry in all mystical things,
and words in their place might move a heart
as players on a stage might recite their part.

Through this eye of the needle, slip your thread
of bare conviction, wetting it not once, but twice
to pierce that hole, for stitching together the whole of you
depends on it, on this sewing of a line in time.

At unease in the world, you assemble the random array:
stones in a circle on a field, coloured sand in a tray.
And when it falls apart—a glorious unbecoming—
you fret in perpetual dismay.

No answer but the question. Your longing is a seed
in search of the light, that luminous centre in which
the self will die, as oblivion and bliss at last unite.

O Anti-phons

A note on "O Anti-phons":

The "O Anti-phons" arose out of an experiment I conducted with poetry and liturgy. The "O Antiphons" are traditionally used during Advent in Western Christian traditions. In the liturgical context, antiphons are short verses from a psalm or anthem sung responsively by choirs or singers in a chant-like manner. I wondered what would happen if I were to write poetry on the antiphons that were not reiterations of them as liturgical pieces intended for worship. Instead, what if I were to respond to them as a contemporary poet struggling with liturgical language and myself as a believer?

O Sapientia

O Wisdom, Who didst come out of the mouth of the Most High,
reaching from end to end and ordering all things mightily and
sweetly: come and teach us the way of prudence.

I wrote on wisdom once when I did not have any.
I wrote on it because I wanted it the way He had it
and not any other way. Wisdom was a longing
I shaped and tipped into a spear; I hurled it
into the sky to hear its keening through the air.

Now I see Wisdom is all around me. Snow.
Dun-feathered creatures pecking at seeds.
A dog taken for a stroll. Squirrel chatter.
Workers on the roof of the church,
still building even when it is so cold.

From end to end, the order in all, mighty and sweet.

O Adonai

Adonai, and Ruler of the house of Israel, Who didst appear unto
Moses in the burning bush, and gavest him the law in Sinai, come
to redeem us with an outstretched arm!

The outstretched arm is what I reach for
in the well of my despair. The law has built
its walls around me. Above is holy light,
that cavernous O the mouth makes out
of the end of a tunnel at which, lo, a bush
appears, burning hot as the sun.

From what have I been redeemed?
The tyranny of self, its lordship of shackles.

For once, I bend at the knee, gaze into the fire,
lose myself properly uttering, *Lord, Lord, Adonai.*

O Radix

Root of Jesse, which standest for an ensign of the people, at Whom
the kings shall shut their mouths, Whom the Gentiles shall seek,
come to deliver us, do not tarry.

O King, shut your mouth, and Christ, take a stand. Root of Jesse,
ensign of the people, plant yourself on the soil of opinion.
O deliver us from ourselves, not expressing
—neither liking nor hating—but seeking.
Come, O Radix, do not tarry!

O Clavis

Key of David, and Sceptre of the house of Israel, that openeth and
no man shutteth, and shutteth and no man openeth, come to
liberate the prisoner from the prison, and them that sit in
darkness, and in the shadow of death.

Two kingdoms, God's and David's, one heavenly, the other earthly;
one key, flesh-shaped, of bone, skin, and hair, unlocks them.
Through Him, entrance. His key also releases fetters
that chain and bind and brings out the prisoner from the cell.
Through Him, Freedom.

But the key also locks out, shuts in, puts away;
it protects, hides, and covets. That book that is chained,
the leaves of His words, remain bound, unfound,
in the chamber of the heart with no keyhole,
no snug aperture in which to fit the instrument.
What then of salvation, to those who know neither lock nor key?
What means the word *liberate* that knows no language,
only darkness and shadow?

O Oriens

Dayspring, Brightness of the everlasting light, Sun of justice, come to give light to them that sit in darkness and in the shadow of death!

O let us begin backwards with darkness and death.
The hour before dawn.
And sit in the shadow of that great self, malingering.
For in winter, the sun is justice and must await its time
like the God who will now enter Time to alter it forever.
Meanwhile, we put up the derrick to extract
from the soul's dark depths
the oil of devotion, that will someday gush out with joy at the
coming brightness of the everlasting light.

O Rex Gentium

King of the Gentiles, yea, and desire thereof! O Cornerstone, that
makest of two one, come to save man, whom Thou hast made out
of the dust of the earth!

You aren't the King of me! Nor boss, nor any kind of Lord.
And yet, what is it I truly desire? I, admittedly, who am dust?
Spit on me, Creator, and make mud out of me! Shape me
into the cornerstone I can and should be.
(But truth be told, if it requires Christ in me
to rule, I cannot bear it!) Woe, that You have made me thus—
high-minded dust that desires, pants, and longs for You
whose very words fell me at the knee,
and wrenches praise out of me,
reluctant as I am, full of angry penury.
O makest of two one!

Epilogue

The Cross Speaks

I was a tree once, and of one body
that extended upwards into the sky
and downwards into the soil.

Many were the seasons of my life,
until it ended with the axe.

Only humans would make out of my death
something out of the death of their God,
my dead body carried by Him
who will die for them.

Still, I will lift Him, and become the tree I once was,
and I will bear Him, as he bore me,
and be planted once more
in the dark soil of my nurturing.

Acknowledgements

Thanks to Alice Major for shaping this manuscript into the book it has become, and to Sharon Caseburg and Melissa Morrow at Turnstone Press for their fine eye for detail in the final stages of editing.

Thanks also to Michiko and Gen Tsuboi, my beloved aunt and uncle. Gen Tsuboi created the art for the cover of this book with the help of Michiko, who translated the titular poem, "Heart's Hydrography" into Japanese.

Thanks to poets Sarah Klassen and Joanne Epp, with whom I have worked extensively on the translation of Catharina Regina von Greiffenberg's devotional sonnets. I have gleaned much inspiration from not only Catharina, but also from Joanne and Sarah's abiding presence and dedication to bringing Catharina's words from German into English.

And finally, thanks be to God, from whom all good things come.

Notes on the Poems

Some of the poems in this book have been previously published in anthologies or journals with some or no alteration. They are as follows: "Idle" in *The Best of The Best Canadian Poetry in English: The Tenth Anniversary Edition,* published by Tightrope Books (2017), "Dervish" in *Writing Menopause: An Anthology of Fiction, Poetry and Creative Nonfiction,* published by Inanna Publications (2017), "Wild Plum" in *Sustenance: Writers from BC and Beyond, on the Subject of Food* published by Anvil Press (2017), "Bleeding Woman" in *GUSH: Menstrual Manifestos for Our Times,* published by Frontenac House (2018), "Evergreens, or the Lordship of the Language" in *Heartwood: Poems for the Love of Trees,* published by The League of Canadian Poets (2018), "Nation of Birds" in *The Emperor's Orphans,* published by Turnstone Press (2018), "Nephesh/Throat" and "Autumn Canopy" in *Prairie Fire* (2013), "For the Atheist" in *The Poet's Quest for God: 21st Century Poems of Faith, Doubt and Wonder,* published by Eyewear Publishing (2016), and "Forge," "Holy Saturday," and "Rooster Song" in *The Society* (2016, 2019, 2020).

"The Cross Speaks" appeared in the art exhibit *Crossings: A Journey to Easter* that was held in Toronto, Ontario from March 2 to April 14, 2022, and appears in the art exhibit catalogue of the same name published in 2022.

The epigraph from Richard Drake on page 81 is from the preface of *A manual of the private devotions and meditations of the Right Reverend Father in God Lancelot Andrews* [sic], *late L. Bishop of Winchester,* published in 1648. I have adapted the quote to have modern spellings of some words.

The last line of "Vesper Sparrow" quotes Juliet Capulet as she waits for her lover Romeo Montague in act 2, scene 2 of William Shakespeare's *Romeo and Juliet*.

The epigraph to "Forge" is by seventeenth-century philosopher William Penn.

The epigraphs to "Albino Hummingbird" and "Bleeding Woman" have been adapted from the World English Bible, https://worldenglish.bible/, which is in the public domain.

The scripture referenced in "Organ" is from the King James Version of the Bible. It, too, is in the public domain.

The italicized text of the "O-Antiphons" are my adaptations of various English translations (of which there are a few) of the original Latin text.